CONFRONTING:
THE KINGDOM OF CULTS, COUNTERFEIT CHRISTIANITY, AND HATEGROUPS

DR. JOHN THOMAS WYLIE

authorHOUSE®

AuthorHouse™
1663 Liberty Drive
Bloomington, IN 47403
www.authorhouse.com
Phone: 1 (800) 839-8640

Published by AuthorHouse   02/06/2018

ISBN: 978-1-5462-2830-1 (sc)
ISBN: 978-1-5462-2829-5 (e)

Print information available on the last page.

CONTENTS

INTRODUCTION

In an attempt to prepare a basic usable publication, I have noted what the gospel says pertaining to (false doctrines): Confronting: "The Kingdom of Cults," "Counterfeit Christianity," and "Hate Groups etc..." In this publication, there are countless other religions and groups besides known "cults" who oppose Christianity and are merely included for study and informative purposes.

As Christians, we must understand the gospel of God's grace and to trust in the living Jesus Christ to aid us when in the presence of the "cultist." The essentials of authentic faith reflected in the following seven questions are designed to help the Christian identify a missionary or representative of the cults. Those questions are:

(1) Do you base your teachings on revelations or sacred writings other than the Bible?

(2) Is your primary task preaching the Gospel of Christ? (see I Cor. 15:3-4). The most important business is proclaiming the Gospel – Is it His? There is no other (Gal. 1:8-9)

(3) Do you believe Jesus is the Messiah, the Christ, the anointed one of God who has come in the flesh (I John 4:1-3)? Is Jesus Of Nazareth the Eternal Word of God become flesh? (See John 1:1,14).

Denial of the Lordship of Christ is the spirit of anti-Christ. (see II John 9)

(4) Do you believe Christ's shed blood is the only basis for the forgiveness of sins?

(see Romans 3:24-25).

(5) Do you believe that Jesus rose from the dead? (see Romans 10:9-10).

(6) Are you personally trusting Jesus Christ as your Redeemer and Lord? The gospel summons every man to trust his risen Redeemer.

(7) Do you depend upon some achievements of your own for your salvation, or is your trust exclusively in the grace of God? (Not by human achievements or doing good. See Romans and Galatians – that salvation is the gift of God's grace, not by works lest any man should boast. See Ephesians 2:8-9. These questions aid one in not only identifying a "cult" but to guide Christians in evangelizing cultists.

Kingdom of Cults: Counterfeit Christianity. What is it? If is not Christianity but a cult.

When our Lord Jesus Christ spoke not only of wars, rumors of wars, famines, pestilences and earthquakes; But Jesus also declared ; "Take heed that no man deceive you. For many shall come in my name, saying, I am Christ; and shall deceive many." And many false prophets shall rise and shall deceive many" (Matthew 24:3-6,11).

Paul states in I Timothy 4:1; 2 Timothy 4:3-4: "Now the spirit speaketh expressly, that in the latter times some shall depart from the faith, giving heed to seducing spirits, and doctrines of devils." "For the time will come when they will not endure sound doctrine; but after their own lusts shall they heap to themselves teachers, having itching ears; and they shall turn away their ears from the truth, and shall be turned unto fables." Counterfeit Christianity (false doctrines, sects, cults, and isms, hate groups, etc... – basically all are counterfeits).

The term "cult" refers to any religious circles or groups who claim to be authorized by Jesus Christ and the Holy Bible. These groups no more worship Jesus Christ than the devil or demons. They may claim the support of the Bible and Jesus Christ, but misses the mark of the high calling of God.

CHAPTER

ONE

CHAPTER

THE

The Kingdom Of Cults: Counterfeit Christianity

A Cult nevertheless misses the heart of Christianity, the "Gospel." The gospel is central in Christianity. It is the gospel that proclaims the good news of Jesus Christ's personal Lordship and atoning work in fulfillment of scriptural prediction. Paul succinctly summarizes the gospel in I Corinthians 15:3-4. Christ died for our sin according to the Scriptures.

Upon this message life is established. Hearing the "good news" a sinner trusts Christ himself and finds spiritual life in union in Him (Eph. 1:13). Furthermore, according to Christ and the apostles, the Old Testament (OT) focuses upon this same gospel (Lk. 24:25-27; 44-47; Acts 10:43), and so does the New Testament (NT) when understood according to sound principles of interpretation.

Confirming this conclusion is the fact that the great doctrinal affirmations through the centuries of church history exalt Jesus Christ crucified for sinners and risen from the dead. Whoever fails to give pre-eminence to the gospel has misse the heart of Christianity (Lewis, 1990).

A cult, then, is any religious movement which claims the backing of Christ of the Bible, but distorts the central message of Christianity by, (1) an additional revelation, and by (2) displacing a fundamental tenet of the faith with a secondary matter (Lewis, 1990).

It is one thing to define "cult" connotatively and another to identify specific groups denoted by the term. Adherents of the cults sincerely claim to be follwers of Christ. The cults have Sunday schools, church services, radio programs, telecasts, revival services, prophetic conferences, Bible correspondence schools, attractives magazines, books, tracts, miralce working power, mission societies, and challenging youth activities. Counterfeits always look genuine (Lewis, 1990).

In her book, "The Great Controversy:" White once stated, "Every conceivable form of error will be accepted by those who willfully reject the truth." Satan has different deceptions prepared to reach different minds; and some who look with horror upon one deception will readily receive another." This is how Satan seduces a mind that is not focused on Jesus Christ (White, 1988).

"Among the most successful agencies of the great deceiver are the delusive doctrines and lying wonders of Spiritualism. Disguised as an angel of light, he (the devil) spreads his nets where least suspected."

"If men would but study the Word of God with earnest prayer that they might understand its teachings, they would not be left in darkness to receive false doctrines. But as they reject the truth, they fall as prey to these (other) doctrines" (White, 1988).

Many cults swear allegniance to Christ but deny the power and workings of the Holy Spirit and His witness. Often time these cults, counterfeit Christian religions, and a host of other counterfeits do not accept the authority of the Bible in full. They may use certain texts of the Bible out of context to promote their causes. Many of these cults (kingdom cults) or so called churches deny essential Christian doctrines at the heart of Christian belief, faith and practice such as:

(1) The Virgin Birth, (2) The Deity of Christ, (3) The Preaching Calvary and The

Blood Atonement, (4) Jesus' Christ Death and Resurrection, (5) The Second Coming of Christ, (6) The Bible as God's Authoritative Word, (7) The Bible as God's Inspired Word, and (8) Everlasting Punishment for the unsaved.

If any religious group, circle, so called church deny any of the foregoing, then persons attending should remove themselves and find a Bible – Believing Chruch (A New Testament Church of Baptized Believers In Christ). There are some who will tell you there is no devil, that such a thought is foolishness in their circles of religion and belief. Satan's greatest tool is to make people believe he does not exist (See Revelation 12:9; 20:3).

Today, there are many groups that state: We accept the Bible, but we have another book which carries equal authority or we have additional books (or other books) with more authority. Such statements are true of the Mormons, Muslims, Jehovah's Witnesses, and Christian Science religions to oname a few. Beloved, I warn you in the sincerest Christian love, there is no other holy book, Save the Bible. The Holy Bible is the Only Word of God (The Gospel).

Why the Bible? Because "the thought of the Bible is the record of wondrous deeds and saving acts of God in history." "The sending of His Son is the mightiest, most climatic act" (Hyatt, 1977).

Another aspect of the definition which seems as equally important is the thought that the Bible is a collection of books which True Christians accept as divinely inspired and as possessing "divine authority." Of these two elements, inspiration and authority – authority is the most distinctive according to the Bible.

This is important because the Bible is an authoritative book. But in order to discover this authority in the Bible, one must come to know God who has revealed Himself through the historical records of the Bible.

It is not sufficient to simply know about God or to have an intellectual understanding of what the Bible says about God. The devil (Satan) and his angels (demons) know that much and tremble in fear for their lives. Rather, one must have a divine, devout, personal, reverential encounter with God through the person of Jesus Christ who is therein revealed to us.

This publication, "Kingdom of Cults: Christian Counterfeits," names and defines a few Counterfeit Christian groups, circles, sects, cults, hate groups, etc... that are a dangerous threat to, and enemies to Christian belief, faith, and practice. These are the tools, keys or devices used by the enemy (devil) to mislead, ensnare, deceive, teach false doctrines through false teachers and false christs. Be well warned and informed that the tampering, dabbling into, joining one's self to, or embracing these ideologies, philosophies, concepts, or isms thereof - are more than strictly forbidden by Jesus Christ our Lord and Savior; and should be avoided.

It is written in the scriptures and inspired of God Himself: "Let no one be found among you who sacrifices his son or daughter in the fire, who practices divination or sorcery, interprets omens, engages in witchcraft, or casts spells, or who is a medium (or spiritualist) or who consults the dead."

"Anyone who does these things is detestable to the Lord, and because of detestable practices the Lord your God will drive out those nations before you." "You must be blameless before the Lord your God (Deuteronomy 18:10-13, NIV)."

"So if anyone tells you, "Thee he is, out in the desert," do not go out; or, "here he is, in the inner rooms,' do not believe it." "For as lightning that comes from the cast is visible even in the west, so will be the Coming of The Son of Man (Matthew 24:24-27).

Religion in the lives of men is always important to Satan." Since mankind is basically religious (he is a religious creature)." Knowing this, Satan must work through that religion." He must find a way to work through Christianity which is not a religion, but a way of holy life in Jesus Christ. If man has the true religion, Satan must sell man on a false religion (or false doctrine)." Then there are no limits to what he may do to that man." Concerning this, I turn to II Timothy 2:26:

The Theory Of Evolution

Although academically, socially, and secularly accepted among most schools, colleges, and universities world – wide, the theory of evolution renders a philosphy which defies, disagrees with, disputes and conflicts with the Biblical accounts of Creation. The famous Harvard Paleontologist, George Gaylord Simpson summarized the result of evolution as "Man is the result of a purposeless and natural process that did not have him in mind."

Charles Robert Darwin, 1809 – 1882, An English Scientist, is accredited with developing the modern theory of evolution, and proposed with Alfred R. White, the principle of natural selection. Darwin published "On The Origin Of Species By Means of Natural Selection" or the Preservation of Favored Faces In the Struggle For Life" 1859, which explained the evolutionary process through natural and sexual arousing great controversy because of its disagreement with the Biblical interpretation of Creation (The Genesis Account).

The Theory of Evolution teaches principles which go farther back than Darwin, Darwin's grandfather, Plato or Aristotle. The philosophy stemming from the theory (principles) has its roots in the devil. We shall identify the theory of evolution briefly and examine its ties to Satan and how it relates to Satan's fall.

The Theory of Evolution:
Historical Background

Although Darwin is generally accredited as the originator of the theory, others existed before Darwin. Thales of Miletus, 640 to 546 B.C. over 2,000 years ago said water developed into simple animals and finally into complex animals like man accord to Thompson, 1981. Since that time evolutionary concepts were passed down to modern times through philosophers such as Plato and Aristotle. It was Darwin's grandfather who devised arguments favoring evolution, but Darwin gave his grandfather no recognition in his own work as once stated by Sunderland in 1998. This reminds me of the devil's (Satan) argument with God and associated with Satan's fall which we shall discuss under the subject" "The Theory of Evolution and Satan's Fall.

A Brief Summary Of The
Theory On Origins Of Life

This theory states, that galaxies, solor systems, stars and planets came into existence as a result of the "BIG BANG." It is believed by chance, our planet being a reasonable distance from the sun had a suitable environment for life to develop. One cell-organisms (simple cells) formed by chemically coming together under the right conditions. Over and extended time simple cells mutated and selection changed. Over a long time frame successful mutations led to development of sea creatures and plants which developed into more complex organisms through the combined process of mutation, adaptation and selection.

Early organisms thought to develop were plants then sponges, jellyfish, starfish, mollusks, worms, insects, crabs and spiders of which later fish, amphibians and reptiles evolved. Reptiles developed into snakes, crocodiles, birds and dinosaurs. Finally, mammals evolved into early man. The whole process took approximately 1,000,000 years according to Baker (Baker, 1996). All this led to life as we know it on planet earth.

The Theory Of Evolution And Satan's Fall

The theory of evolution and Satan's fall can be briefly summed up with the writings and interpretations rendered in the words of Dr. Gordon Lindsay on Henry Morris's explanation on the origin of the Theory of Evolution associated with the Fall of Satan.

In Dr. Lindsay's book, "Satan's Rebellion And Fall," we find an explanation via H. M. Morris: "Evolution did not owe its orgin with Charles Darwin. The Doctrine of spontaneous generation was generally believed by the ancients. The idea of creation by an Omnipotent God is almost unique and is found only by revelation of the Holy Scriptures (Lindsay, 1972).

The theory in some form or other, more of less than is how can we explain such a wide spread belief in a theory that is so contrary to scientific evidence? The answer is found in II Corinthians 4:3-4. "But if our Gospel be hid, it is hid to them that are lost: In whom the god of this world hath blinded the minds of them which believe not, lest the light of the glorious gospel of Christ, who is the image of God, should shine unto them."

This, it is that Satan has blinded the minds of men so that they have sought some plausible explanation of the universe as an alternative to the Biblical Account of Creation. If it could be proved that men have evolved through the evolutionary process of nature, they owe no allegiance to a Creator. They are not of a fallen race; they need no redemption (Lindsay, 1972).

Satan being the father of lies, has originated this monsterous falsehood through the centuries. As we analyze the matter, we see that the truth of falsity of the theory of evolution becomes the one and basic issue that mankind faces.

It is the matter of whether or not God is the Sovereign Ruler of the universe, and that man does or does not owe Him absolute allegiance (Lindsay, 1972).

All religions except Christianity are made more or less creature – centered. They all revolved around some system in which man may better himself, rather than submit himself to the grace of God by which alone is salvation (Lindsay, 1972).

This brings up the question of how Satan came to fall in the first place. We are told he was "the anointed cherub that covereth and at one time was perfect." "Thine heart was lifted up because of thy beauty, thou hast corrupted thy wisdom by reason of thy brightness" (Ezekiel 28:17). Isaiah further informs us that Satan rebelled against God – saying in his heart: "I will ascend into heaven; I will exalt my throne above the stars of God... I will be like the Most High" (Isaiah 14:13-14).

The question is why did Satan allow pride to come into his heart and deceive him into believing that he could displace God from His throne. God had told him that he was a created being (Ezekiel 28:13-15). But apparently, there came a time when doubt entered into his mind that this was really so (Lindsay, 1972).

The only evidence he had was that God hath told him this was true. Morris points out Satan's reasonings: "Could it not be that both he and God had come into existence in some way unknown and that it was just an accident of priority in time that enabled God to exercise control? With all his beauty and wisdom, Satan could undoubtedly win the allegiance of many other angels who had similar reason to question the Word of God (Lindsay, 1972).

But how could Satan possibly rationalize this notion that both he and God and all the other beings had come into existence in similar fashion and, therefore, were essentially of the same order? If God had not created him, who had? If God were not All-Powerful, who was?

In other words, who was really God? The only possible answer that could be given by Satan which could in any way rationalize his rebellion was there was really no creator at all! Somehow, everything must have come about by a process of material growth, of development of evolution.

If he would not believe the Word of God, then this is what he must believe. And this is what he still believes! For, despite the clear testimony of the Word of God concerning his ultimate defeat and eternal punishment he still refuses to believe that it is really so, and so he continues to rebel and hope that he will ultimately be victorious in this conflict of the ages (Lindsay, 1972).

Certainly, the philosophy of Satan was what he essentially presented to Eve in the garden. He implied that God's Word was not to be trusted; but God was withholding knowledge from them (Adam and Eve) which they had a right to have. If Eve would obey him by taking of the forbidden fruit, she would not die but be as "gods" knowing both good and evil." Satan's philosophy was that there were other gods besides God.

The drift of the antediluvian civilization was away from God to the exaltation of man as man makes his own destiny. The story of the tragic apostasy of the human race is told in Romans 1:21-25. Men became vain in their imaginations and their foolish heart was darkened. Who changed the truth of God into a lie, and worshiped and served the creature more than the Creator wo is bless forever, Amen.

Evolution in other words is pointless. It sees creation creating itself; therefore, there is no need for a "Creator." So men resist the thought that they are morally accountable, and that God will come some day in judgment. As the Apostle Peter said: "Where is the promise of His Coming? For since the fathers fell asleep, all things continue as they were from the beginning of creation (2 Peter 3:3-4).

Thus, it appears that all evil in the universe has had its genesis in some kind of idea of evolution in which all things have come to be through the process of nature instead of through the direct creative act of God. It is the principles of man asserting his sovereignty against the sovereignty of God.

CHAPTER

TWO

Counterfeit Christianity
(The Cults)

The term "cult" is used which may be rendered as "Counterfeit Christianity," want to be christian, but are without Christ. Their so called churches are not churches although they have a Bible, often use the name of Jesus Christ and often believing He is not God; or that they themselves are a sort of deity.

A Cult may be defined as a system or community of religious worship and ritual, especially one focusing upon a single deity or spirit. Obsessive devotion or veneration for a person, principle or ideal. The object of such devotion. An exclusive group of persons sharing an esoteric interest (The American Heritage Dictionary Of The English Language, 1982).

Recognize No Other gospel

Numerous who say they trust Christ likewise put their trust in some human achievements to legitimacy avocation. This gives a false representation of their affirmed confidence. The entire book of Romans and Galatians attest that such have missed the main gospel. Ephesians 2:8-9 announces that salvation is the endowment of God's elegance, not of works for fear that any man ought to brag.

The endeavor to recognize the heart of Christianity from cultic depravities is made, not to disparage any individual or association, but rather affectionately to indicate swindled people or individuals the core of uncovered truth. The particular focuses are underlined in light of the fact that they are made of express in the Bible itself.

It is the Bible which says we should perceive no other gospel, recognize that Jesus is the Christ, have confidence in his blood, trust that He was raised from the dead, believe Him and depend not all alone works. What the Bible unequivocally requires of the way of confidence and its items, Christians request. Christians must perceive as "cultic" all who uproot these doubtlessly uncovered truths for something else, however praiseworthy a less focal matter might be.

The seven inquiries situated in the acquaintance serve with recognize a faction as well as to guide Christians in evangelizing cultists. With that positive objective in view the cross examinations diagram consequent investigations of individual factions. Focusing the dialogs upon fundamentals, these questions additionally encourage similar examinations of cultic educating on the particular subjects (Lewis, 1975).

Why Cults Thrive

"Why the doctrinal contrasts," Christians are enticed to state, "the factions must have something or they would not develop so quick! What would we be able to gain from the astonishing advancement of the factions?" Here are a portion of the informational purposes behind development of the cliques.

(1) Instead of accentuating lecturing and love, the factions stretch instructing and preparing each part to end up plainly a teacher of the clique development. They are principally concerned not to engage their individuals candidly every week, but rather to send them into the world seven days seven days as forceful and profitable delegates.

(2) Every part is relied upon to do way to

entryway appearance. The Jehovah's witnesses have a standard calendar of a stipulated number of hours seven days. Mormon youngsters are relied upon to give a year or two of their lives at their own cost to their preacher movement.

(3) Prospective individuals are given home Bible classes. Such rehashed visits conquer hindrances and address individual issues. Frequently they create enduring believers from the home as well as from the area in which they are held.

(4) Attractive religion writing is accessible to advocates in mass amounts at most practical rates. Jehovah's witness distribute Awake, a 30-page paper like clockwork in 23 dialects and 3,250,000 duplicates. Likewise semi-month to month in their Watchtower Magazine which turns out in 61 dialects and 3,800,000 duplicates. The exceedingly respected Christen Science Monitor incorporates its day by day tract in support of the development, and Christian Science Reading Rooms stacked with writing dab each real city.

(5) New prospects are picked up from radio and TV communicates which present such

excellent elements as the Mormon Choir and Temple organ.

(6) Many a huge number of individuals past their own enrollments are educated cultic regulation through correspondence courses. In the interim zealous houses of worship regularly can't invigorate their own particular individuals to genuine book of scriptures study.

(7) The support of scholarly organizations is progressively apparent among the factions. In Utah Mormons guarantee one of the finest instructive frameworks America can brag. The Seventh Day Adventists, if named a religion, additionally set up their own particular schools to prepare kids from the earliest starting point in their unmistakable convictions.

(8) obviously it takes conciliatory giving for broad structures, radio and TV programming, tremendous amounts of writing, and scholarly overhead! Tithing has had a noteworthy impact in the exceptional development of Mormonism and Seven Day Adventists. Their yearly per capita livelihoods tower far over those of non-tithing gatherings. Is it not abnormal that those obliged by law to give a tenth accomplish more

than the individuals who radiance in limitless beauty?

(9) Furthermore the numerous exercises of the factions are channeled to all inclusive human needs. Case: Mormons actualize a social worry with solid projects so they can gloat that none of their families is ever in need. The impression might be given that standard chapels are unconcerned Pharisees who cruise the penniless by, while the cliques exhibit great Samaritan empathy.

(10) Concern for well-being joined by guaranteed cures turns out to be a viable mix for Christian Science and other recuperating religions.

(11) Add to this the way that the cliques furnish their supporters with a basic code of life rather than a perplexing labyrinth of urgings. They realize what is anticipated from them and the reasonable requests can be met.

The Christian Attitude Towards Cults

It has been normal for Christians to disregard the factions and grin as though they were moderately irrelevant and unworthy of thought.

As the religions surge ahead this "head in the sand" state of mind turns out to be less agreeable (Lewis, 1975). The congregation endures substantial loses a seemingly endless amount of time on account of the altogether assault upon it by the religions. Mindful of the supported effect of the cliques upon Christendom, no dedicated steward of the Gospel of Christ can stay unconcerned (Lewis, 1975).

Numerous Christians appear to be happy with an invalidation of cultic teaching and judgment of the developments. Be that as it may, Christians are dependable to proselytize betrayed individuals in the factions. Are not we like Paul indebted individuals to all men (Rom. 1:14)? Do we not owe declaration of the gospel to the religious and in addition the unreligious? Indeed, even today Christians should pay their obligations!

Is an endeavor to proselytize individuals from the factions an exercise in futility? Not if the gospel is as yet the energy of God unto salvation to everybody that believeth (Rom. 1:16)! There might be blasphemers in the cliques, however even they merit two counsels before swinging thoughtfulness regarding others (Titus 3:10). Among the cultists there may likewise be renegades - individuals who have previously sworn devotion to Christ as uncovered in Scripture and who have purposely and for all time dismisses the observer of the Holy Spirit to the Savior.

We can't be certain beyond a shadow of a doubt that these conditions have been satisfied even with broad learning of a person. Be that as it may, the heft of present day cultists have experienced childhood in their developments failing to have made whatever other duty. They are meriting the gospel as Jews, Hindus, Muslims, Buddists, Confucianists, Shintoists, Taoism, or despise gatherings.

Are individuals from the cliques excessively troublesome, making it impossible to win for Christ? They are for minor men, yet not for the Holy Spirit. Paul guaranteed Timothy that God will give apology and recuperation out of the catch of the fallen angel to some who are abducted by Satan at his will (II Timothy 2:25-26). Does this exclude individuals and even pioneers of the factions? On the off chance that the master can change Muslims, is a Jehovah's Witness too hard for Him? He who changed an over the top Saul into preacher Paul does not shudder at seeing a cultist.

Be that as it may, God has achieved cultists as others through human instruments. "By what method should they hear without a minister" (Romans 10:14)? An immense and poor mission field lies at our doorstep; the universe of the religions is white unto gather.

Christians should be steadfast in seeing. Christians will keep away from silly and unlearned inquiries, however they set out not neglect to ask the forever imperative inquiries recorded in this production. They will help guide individuals far from false accounts to the Gospel of Christ.

CHAPTER

THREE

Jehovah's Witnesses

Individuals from a "religious" association starting in the United States under the initiative of Charles Taze Russell, 1852-1916. Jehovah's Witness anticipated Christ's Second Coming in 1914, and in all witness trust it is inescapable. All witness are relied upon to partake in house-to-house lecturing; there is no ministry. Jehovah's Witness accept just 144,000 picked adherents will reign with Christ in paradise; yet earth will keep on existing as home to whatever is left of mankind.

Witnesses trust they ought not end up noticeably required in the issues of the world, and their fundamentals, including dismissal of commitments, for example, military administration, have regularly carried them into strife with expert (Lewis, 1990).

Most, as sources differing uncover - don't trust Jesus as "Godliness" (Deity of Christ, The Godhead of Christ). While Jehovah Witnesses are valid on lessons of Christ's mankind, they neglect to represent the immense proof in sacred writing that Christ is God (Lewis, 1990).

"In opposition to the claim of Jehovah's

Witnesses, at that point, the Bible not disregarding Jesus' humankind, and peculiarity from the father, additionally shows His basic divinity." In John 1, the Word who moved toward becoming substance (v.14) and who was endlessly "with God (v.1)... is additionally pronounced to be God (v.1).

In the New World Translation, nonetheless, Jehovah Witnesses change the finish of verse one so it peruses, "the Word was a divine being." The little "g" is required, they contend, in light of the fact that the Greek word for God (Theos, from which we get the word Theology) is not gone before by an unequivocal article, "the" (ho). "At the point when this contention is introduced, any Christian as intrigued as Jehovah's Witness laymen can call attention to three things:

To begin with, it ignores totally a built up lead of Greek syntax which necessities the rendering .... what's more, the word was God .... A distinct predicate. It doesn't have the article when it goes before the verb" .... In the last condition of John 1:1 the predicate nominative "God" goes before the verb "was." That request accentuates Christ's divinity, and clarifies the nonattendance of the distinct article. Since English words arrange vary from Greek, the expression is deciphered, "The Word was God..." (Lewis, 1990).

In the second place any Christian can bring up to Jehovah's Witness that the Word for "God" (Theos) without the unequivocal article ("the") is frequently utilized for Jehovah God. He may demonstrate this to an observer in the New World Translation, "Theos" without the articles of God, with a capital "G" in John 1:6,12,13,; 3:2, 21!

Third, any Christian can demonstrate a Jehovah Witness the way that a few entries do assign Jesus as God, utilizing the unmistakable articles (ho) with God (Theos). As per Matthew 1:23, the introduction of Jesus satisfied the prophetic declaration that the virgin birth (virgin conceived child), ought to be called "Immanuel," which implies when deciphered, "With us is God" or "God With Us." Not the capital "G" which as per the New World Translators, means Jehovah God, the God, ho theos (Lewis, 1990).

The Scriptures, uncover the Word progressed toward becoming fragile living creature and stay among us (incarnate). Jehovah Witnesses trust

"Jesus" birth on earth was not an incarnation... He exhausted himself for goodness' sake magnificent and spiritual...... he was conceived a man. He was not dressed with substance..: "Despite the fact that the witnesses acknowledge the principle of virgin birth, they keep up that Jesus was only human until submersed at thirty years old.

For the witnesses, Jesus, some time recently, and after His gritty presence, was the most noteworthy otherworldly animal, and amid life on earth was an immaculate man; Jesus was never really God. The Bible, they say, does not educate the god of Christ.

Once more, when suspicious Thomas was at long last overpowered with the confirmation that Jesus had become alive once again, he shouted out, "My Master and My God:" (John 20:28). The Jehovah's Witnesses possess interpretation utilizes a capital "G". Their sacred writings unmistakeably call Jesus, Jehovah God, the God (ho theos). Moreover, a similar adaptation speaks to Jesus as tolerating the love of Thomas and praising all who share his confidence. "Jesus said to Him: "Since you have seen me have you trusted?" Happy are the individuals who don't see but accept (v.29, New World Translation)."

In Hebrews 1:8, Jesus who is higher than the blessed messengers, is called God (ho theos). "Unto the Son He saith, Thy royal position O God is for ever and ever." However, the witnesses reword the verse, they can scarcely evade the connection with Psalm 45:6-7 where it is Jehovah's energy in a path in which no celestial animal is.

In his first Epistle, the witness John, having discussed Christ affirms, "He (Literally "this one, a manly individual pronoun concurring with the previous Christ) Christ is the True God and Eternal Life (I John 5:20, Lewis, 1990).

A few different entries suggest as much by calling Jesus "God our Savior" (I Timothy 1:1; 2:3; 4:10; Titus 1:3; 2:10;3:4). In different verses the expressions "Jesus" and "God": are so linguistically related as to educate their basic solidarity." Although disregarded by the New World Translators, this Greek structure was distinguished and planned by Granville Sharp as long prior as A.D. 1798. Sharp's run applies when two things of a similar case associated by the Greek connecting (Kai signifying "and") have an article going before the First thing and no article before the second thing.

In such a development the second thing dependably alludes to an indistinguishable thing or occasion from the first. In this way II Thessalonians 1:12 discusses the finesse of Our God and Lord Jesus Christ. Titus 2:13 alludes to the showing up of Our Great God and Lord Jesus Christ; and II Peter 1:1 implies the honorableness of Our God and Savior Jesus Christ. In each of the sections Jesus is related to God" (Lewis, 1990).

In the event that additional proof is called for concerning Christ's Deity, watch that celestial credits are attributed to Him. Christ is Eternal (Micah 5:2; Hebrews 1:11, Omnipresent - John 3:13; Matthew 18:20; Ephesians 1:23. Omniscient - John 1:48; 2:25; 6:64; 16:30; 21:17; Colossians 2:3. Transcendent - Matthew 28:18; Hebrews 1:3; and Sinless - John 8:46; I Peter 1:19.

Heavenly nature Works credited to Christ are confirmation of His Deity as takes after: Creation - John 1:3; Colossians 1:16; Preservation - Colossians 1:17, Providence - Hebrews 1:3; Forgiveness - check 2:5-11; Luke 5:20-24, and Judgment - John 5:22; James 4:12.

On the off chance that Jesus were not God at that point love of Him would be Idolatrous, "love and administration of the animal instead of the Creator" (Romans 1:25)! Be that as it may, since Jesus Christ is God, Jehovah's Witnesses are jeopardizing their everlasting predetermination. The Scripture says, "On the off chance that you don't trust that I Am He, You will kick the bucket in you sins" John 8:24.

The Resurrection Of Christ

A question identifying with the perfection of Christ's life may help a cultist to see the genuine establishment of Christianity. Ask, "Do you trust that Jesus Christ became alive once again?" If the reaction is agreed, ask for a clarification. What is implied by "restoration"?

As indicated by Jehovah's Witnesses the restoration of Jesus does not imply that the body which was executed and covered lived once more. Their significant content edits, "Jehovah God raised him from the dead, not as a human Son, but rather as a compelling improper soul Son.... "He being killed in the substance, however being made alive in the soul'" (1 Peter 3:;18 NWT). Before turning into a man He was a soul being; presently, after the perish of the individual, the soul being exists once more. "Minister Russel obviously stated, "The man Jesus is dead, everlastingly dead." What happened to the body of our Lord?" Russel answers:

Our Lord's human body was.... extraordinarily expelled from the tomb; in light of the fact that had it stayed there it would have been an unrealistic obstruction to the confidence of the disciples.... We don't know anything about what was the fate of it, with the exception of that it didn't rot or degenerate (Acts 2:27, 31). Regardless of whether it was broken down into gasses or whether it is as yet protected some place as the stupendous remembrance of God's affection ..... nobody knows."

How at that point does the shrewd "Minister" clarify the revival appearances of Christ to the devotees? How could "an undetectable soul animal" be noticeable? When seeking to show up Christ "in a split second made and expected such an assortment of fragile living creature and such attire as He saw fit for the reason proposed.." When the appearance was finished a similar otherworldly power "broke up" them. Later Witnesses call the appearances "emergence (Lewis, 1990).

The focal issue between Christian ideas of the restoration and those of the Witnesses is not whether there were appearances of the body in which He passed on and in which He in this way showed up. "Numerous Christians have the thought," Russell expresses, "that our Lord's radiant otherworldly body is the exceptionally same body that was executed and laid away in Joesph's tomb: they expect, when they see the Lord in brilliance, to recognize him by the scars he got on Calvary. This is an extraordinary slip-up." (Lewis, 1990).

Are Christians mixed up in stating a personality between the killed and risen Christ? Somewhere in the range of have a tendency to concur that they are. Is the revival body altogether different from the regular body. As per I Corinthians 15 the body raised from the dead is eternal, morally sound, respectable, effective, otherworldly, glorious, and heavenly.

The revival body is as unique in relation to the transient body as full-developed grain from the seed that is planted (I Cor. 15:37). This is valid. In the meantime, in any case, there is a proceeding with character seed that is sown and the grain that creates. This need not suggest that indistinguishable particles create the modest seed and the high stalks.

The cells of human bodies change no less than at regular intervals, yet their natural personality is continuous. Is not such a natural personality traceable in the killed and risen Lord?

In both pre-and post-torturous killing states, Christ's body was noticeable, substantial, and capable of being heard. He could eat with his devotees. Exceptionally particular was "the print of the nails" (Jn. 20"25,27 NWT).

At the point when Christians attest that the revived Christ was not just a soul animal (holy messenger) they are not mixed up; they essentially rehash a truth from the lips of their Lord.

It is not the Christians who are mixed up in recognizing the killed and unceasingly lifted up Lord; the individuals who think they will forever laud a soul animal (heavenly attendant) who did not drain and bite the dust for their wrongdoings "are of all men most to be pitied"!!!

In the event that the Jesus who kicked the bucket is not raised up from the dead, their proclaiming "is unquestionably futile." their "confidence is futile," and they are still in their transgressions (I Cor. 15:12-19).

CHAPTER

FOUR

The Unification Church:
(The Moonies)

"The Unification Church or The "Moonies" (a cult) was founded in Korea in 1954 by the Sun Myung Moon. The number of members is about 200,000 world-wide via 1992 statistics approximately. Their theology unites Christian and Taoist ideas and is based on Moon's book, "The Divine Principle" which teaches that the original purpose of creation was to set up a perfect family in a perfect relationship with God (Webster's New World Encyclopedia, 1992).

This was thwarted by the fall of Man, and history is seen as a continuous attempt to restore the original plan, now said to have found its fulfillment in the reverend and Mrs. Moon. The Unification Church teaches marriage is essential for spiritual fulfillment, and marriage partners are sometimes chosen for members by reverend moon, although individuals are free to reject a chosen partner. Marriage, which takes the form of mass blessings by reverend and Mrs. Moon, is the "most important ritual" of the church; it is preceded by the wine or engagement ceremony.

There are a few other rituals, although there

is a weekly pledge, which is a ceremony or re-dedication. Accusations that the church engages in a cult (which it is) – like programming of members, and its business, political, and journalistic activities have given it a persistently controversial and derogatory reputation (Webster's New World Encyclopedia, 1992).

Today, the Moonies (Unification Church) are numbered at approximately 2 million members worldwide in about 120 countries. Reverend Moon claims to be "The Christ" (This of course, is a lie!)

The Sacred scriptures are the "divine principle" (a reinterpretation of The Bible with influences of Buddhism, Taosim, and Islam) of Moon, outline of the principle, and the Bible which is used to be made a "Mockery of It!" a few basic beliefs of the moonies are as follows:

The Moonies Belief About Jesus Christ

The moonies trust it appears that Jesus was an impeccable man, yet "He is not God." He was the charlatan posterity of Zechariah and Mary, and the "Cross:" is an image of the annihilation of Christianity. Jesus accomplished otherworldly salvation, yet He neglected to achieve physical salvation.

He didn't revive physically nor resurrect from the grave. They show that Jesus mission was to join Jews, locate a flawless lady of the hour, and start an impeccable family, however He fizzled; and now comes Moon.

CHAPTER

FIVE

The Church Of The Latter Day Saints
(Mormons)

Mormonism is a lifestyle honed by individuals from the Church of Jesus Christ of contemporary Saints, frequently called Mormons or Latter Day Saints. In spite of the fact that the congregation's enrollment is packed in the Western piece of the United States particularly Utah, individuals are likewise found somewhere else in the United States (Lexicon Universal Encyclopedia, 1983).

Joseph Smith established the congregation in Fayette, N.Y., in 1830. Prior he detailed having dreams of God and other sublime creatures in which he was informed that he would be the instrument to set up the reestablished Christian church. As indicated by Smith, one of the great envoys guided him to some thin metal plates, gold in appearance and engraved in a hieroglyphic dialect. Smith;s interpretation of the plates, the Book Of Mormon, depicts the history, wars, and religious convictions of a gathering of individuals (c600BC-AD 421) who moved from Jerusalem to America.

Smith pulled in a little gathering of supporters who settled in Kirkland, Ohio, and

Jackson County, Mo. Due to mistreatment the congregation moved to northern Missouri and after that to Nauvoo, Ill. In 1837 preachers were sent to England and later to Scandinavia; the vast majority of their believers emigrated to the United States (Lexicon Universal Encyclopedia, 1983).

Feeling crested June 1844, when a furnished horde killed Smith, who had been imprisoned in Chicago, Ill. Brigham Young, the leader of the congregation's board of the Twelve Apostles, was voted pioneer of the congregation at an uncommon gathering on August 8, 1846. He composed and coordinated the epic walk from Nauvoo, Ill. over the fields and mountains to the Great Salt Basin.

In Utah the congregation kept on becoming yet was tested by the U.S. government on account of the affirmation of polygamy as a Mormon fundamental. A War practically grew, yet Mormon pioneers chosen to bargain after just sporadic battling. In 1890 the Mormons formally finished the act of plural marriage (Lexicon Universal Encyclopedia, 1983).

Divine Authority Acknowledged...But

Do you construct your convictions in light of disclosures or sacrosanct compositions other than the Bible?

Mormons recognize the celestial specialist, of the Bible, as well as of the Book of Mormon, The Doctrine and Covenants, The Pearl Of Great Price, and nonstop disclosure in the official instructing of the President of the congregation. Taking after author Joseph Smith's "Articles of Faith (8,9) they say, "We trust the Bible to be the expression of God to the extent it is interpreted effectively; we additionally trust the Book of Mormon to be the expression of God. We trusted all that God has uncovered, and all that He does now uncover and we trust that He will yet uncover numerous awesome and critical things relating to the Kingdom of God (Lewis, 1990)."

Where do Mormons search for these future disclosures? Due to their teaching of persistent disclosure Latter-day Saints have solid words for Christians who demand that the Bible is the adequate and just reliable control of confidence and practice. Smith, in the Book of Mormon, calls such Christians "Gentiles: and fools,..." (Lewis, 1990).

The Mormons have been deceived in adding different books to the Biblical disclosure. For a certain something, Mormons are not the only one in guaranteeing proceeded with disclosure. Christian Science include Mary Baker Eddy's Science and Health with key to the Scriptures to the Bible; the Muslims have their Koran; and Spiritualists think their rehashed seances deliver messages from the other world.

Nobody can be required to acknowledge all these indicated disclosures without thought. Furthermore, why would it be a good idea for us to be positively arranged toward Latter Day Saints disclosures?

Troublesome without a doubt is the undertaking of one who tries to orchestrate the proclaiming of Mormon disclosure on any given subject. Polygamy, for instance is both directed and censured. As per one endeavor to translate this matter with some consistency the Mormons say polygamy as a licentious practice is denounced, yet men had passed on and it was important to repopulate "zion." yet it was on July 12, 1843, in Nauvoo, Illinois, that

Joseph Smith got the "disclosure" concerning polygamy.

The exhausting voyage to Utah had not yet incurred significant injury! Others propose that the disagreement is blended on the off chance that we understand the "interminable agreement" with its orderly polygamy still stands. The contract makes the practice interminable when it says, "If ye withstand not in that pledge at that point are ye accursed" (Doctrines and Covenants 132)(Lewis, 1990).

The Gospel

Is the present Church of Jesus Christ of modern Saints now giving pre-distinction to the gospel? At least one of Mormonism's different aspects which emerge from changed sources may usurp the essential place of the gospel (Lewis, 1990).

From Roman Catholicism comes the accentuation upon a progression head not by a pope but rather a president who communicates display day divine revelations to man. The Campbellites recommended the idea of submersion recovery which prompts interest with absolution for the dead. Judaism is reflected in a conspicuous organization and distraction with legalistic works. Smith's and Young's encounters with Masonry gave thoughts of mystery imagery and sanctuary services (Lewis, 1990).

The thought of polygamy and blood penance (by men now), and additionally of present day prophet, originated from Islam. Mohammed inspired Joseph Smith that he assigned hims "the present day Mohammed." And the Rosicrucian regulation that men are divine beings in developing life started Smith's hypothesis that "As a man seems to be, God once was, as God may be, man may progress toward becoming (Lewis, 1990).

Christ

At the heart of the Biblical gospel is the teaching of the divinity and incarnation of Jesus Christ. Assume you inquire as to whether the trusts these truths. "Do you trust that Jesus Christ, the blessed Messiah, who was God (Jn. 1:1) and moved toward becoming substance (Jn. 1:14)?" What answer is a Mormon liable to give?

Mormons don't show His divinity in a Trinitarian sense. Christ is not the Son of God as Orthodox Christians have comprehended the Scripture, yet a "soul offspring of God" as every single individual should have been before their introduction to the world.

Whenever God, "the most shrewd" of the interminable insights, chosen to dress the others with otherworldly shape, Christ was the primary sired. Christ was not endlessly the Father's Son; He was not interminably pre-famous. He "was the Firstborn Spirit Child, and from that day forward he has had, in every way, the pre-greatness." Clearly at that point, Mormons don't show that Christ was basically one with the Father, or that He was God. Also, they will change Scripture which shows Christ's genuine divinity.

Their treatment of John 1:1 is like that of the Jehovah's Witnesses. Congressperson Wallace F. Bennett in his book, Why I Am A Mormon, with the doctrinal "imprimatur" of the President of the L.D.S. Washington Stake, says, "We would read it this: before all else was Jesus, and Jesus was with God, and Jesus was (a) God." (Lewis, 1990).

Jehovah's Witnesses, having faith in just a single God, print "a divine being" with a little letter "g"; Mormons trusting in numerous Gods, decipher it with a capital "G." But by embeddings "a" preceding "God" both prevent the genuine god from claiming Jesus Christ who is forever and basically one with the Father and the Spirit. John 1:1 still stands! "The Word was God." (Lewis, 1990).

In any case, all such acclaim of Christ as redemmer misses the mark concerning Christian instructing. In the event that Jesus was not the Son of one genuine God, He can't spare. Also, what is this "board of the Gods"? They are three independently and physically particular Gods, as indicated by Mormon Apostle Talmadge.

At that point in straight denying the principle of the Trinity, Talmadge includes, "This can't normally be contrued to imply that the Father, the Son, and the Holy Ghost are one in substance.

Why is the solidarity of the Godhead silly to Talmadege and different Mormons alike? Two, not to mention three, material things can't possess a similar space in the meantime! What's more, "Conceding the identity of God, we are constrained to acknowledge the reality of His materiality." Why so? At that point it winds up plainly difficult to comprehend the identity of "insights," "soul kids," "unembodied spirits," and the Holy Spirit! By the by they show that the Father and Son, if not the Holy Spirit, have "strict fragile living creature and-bone bodies (Lewis, 1990)."

Redemption

Another vital question: "Do you trust Christ's blood is the main reason for the pardoning of sins?" An answer the Mormon may give is that as brilliant as might be the all inclusive advantages of Christ's compensation, it is of little benefit for the ordinary living Mormon! Christ's passing is not the premise of his absolution.

Christ's work just opens the entryway; man's work must do the rest. Christ makes the initial installment; Mormons must make installments the greater part of their lives.

For Momons, at that point, the compensation was not totally given by Christ. Senior Bruce R. McConkie scorns the Christian conviction that salvation is not on the ground of human legitimacy, but rather of Christ's legitimacy alone.

Obviously the principle of avocation by confidence on the value of Christ's work alone can be contorted. Be that as it may, the confidence that legitimizes is likewise the confidence that works in adoration (Gal. 5:6). Whoever holds that the expiation work of Christ gave just a chance to individuals to accomplish their own particular salvation has missed the heart of the Christian message.

Mormons, as urgently as others, have to know about the uplifting news of the legitimization by confidence. It gives (1) exculpate from all transgression and (2) the ideal nobility of Jesus Christ. A Mormon who acknowledges the educating of his congregation neglects to understand that keeping laws (regardless of the possibility that called the laws of the gospel) never has been the premise of anybody's exemplary nature in seeing God.

The Scriptures proclaim: "By the deeds of the law there should no substance be advocated in his sight; by the law is the information of transgression" (Romans 3:20). The exemplary nature the Bible educates is "without," or separated from the law (Romans 3:21). Devotees are legitimized "unreservedly by his beauty through the recovery that is in Jesus Christ: Whom God hath put forward to be an appeasement through confidence in his blood" (Rom. 3:24-25). Not simply Christians, but rather the Scriptures show that men are exculpated, God's law fulfilled, and God's rage satisfied, by acknowledgment of the finished compensation of Christ. Mormons accept there is no salvation outside of their clerics or their overlap!

The works of Mormon ministers are not any more ready to save than those of Israel's clerics! (Of Believers to Christ not law managers; see Hebrews 10:17-18). The Mormons are much similar to the Israelites of old (see 10:1).

The Resurrection Of Christ

A vital state of salvation, as indicated by Romans 10:9-10, is conviction that Jesus was raised from the dead. Do Mormons admit Christ's restoration? They do. Talmadge well says:

"The actualities of Christ's restoration from the dead are authenticated by such a variety of scriptural verifications that undoubtedly of the truth discovers put in the brain of any adherent to the motivated records."

In support of this announcement the standard writings are recorded and supplemented with citations from other Mormon "disclosures," The considerable accentuation in Latter-day Saint compositions falls on Christ's revival as the principal products of the restoration of all men (Alma 33:22).

Appreciative not to discover an issue now. Christians will continue all the more ideally to the rest of the inquiries.

Personal Trust

Faith includes scholarly consent to Christ's divinity, passing, and restoration. In any case, it includes more than that. The gospel's truths, similar to a hotly anticipated enrolled letter, convey to us something exceptionally important. By the Spirit of God they convey the living Christ to a heathen.

A Mormon who takes after the educating of his religion ought to have no wavering in attesting that the has a fundamental duty. For Mormonism, with respect to zealous

Christianity, faith is not minor conviction, "only scholarly consent," or "detached as an understanding or acknowledgment as it were." Rather, confidence (Faith) is dynamic, positive, "vivified, vitalized, living conviction." It takes after that confidence in a uninvolved sense, that is, as negligible faith in the more shallow feeling of the term, is wasteful as a methods for salvation."

With this dynamic perspective of confidence (faith), Christians generously concur. Be that as it may, little is by all accounts written in Mormon writing about association with the Living Lord.

Singular Mormons appear to be identified with God just through the reflection of the institutional church and its holy observances. Since Latter-day Saints may not know the delight of individual fellowship with God through the one go between, Jesus Christ (I Tim. 2:5). Christians may help altogether now by relating their own understanding of association with Christ.

Include too the observer of a develop Mormon who for a long time contemplated the Bible while get ready to show religious philosophy in a L.D.S. Help Society. Carolyn J. Sexauer, in "My Testimony of the Grace of God," composes: (fractional letter):

"I left Mormonism." Since that brilliant day when I surrendered attempting to accommodate the lessons of Mormonism with the Word of God, as found in the Bible, as might have been "conceived again" of the Spirit, I have been more joyful than any time in recent memory in my life, and have known in full measure "the tranquility of God that passeth all understanding."

"I experience every day cheering. Each weight on my heart is no more. Each uncertainty and dread is no more."

In perspective of declarations like this, a Mormon who cases to have a crucial confidence in Christ may not in reality have encountered recovery. He might be confiding in just in Christ, additionally in his own particular works. He might be seen this by the following question.

Faith Alone

"Do you rely on upon your very own few accomplishments for avocation or do you rest upon God's elegance gotten through confidence alone?" Here a Mormon will take clear special case. He may even call the convention of avocation by confidence a noxious blunder.

One miracles if the Mormon assault on the convention of legitimization by confidence alone depends on understanding it. The cartoon of the teaching criticized by Talmadge is not educated by the Christian church.

As an author of the standard doctrinal content of Mormonism puts it, "legitimization by conviction alone" is "a most malevolent regulation."

Indeed it is. However, Christianity has never declared a creed such that "a tedious calling of conviction might open the entryways of paradise to the miscreant." The penance of Christ alone opens the entryways of paradise.

A delinquent who by confidence recognizes himself with Christ is legitimized, not by what he has done, but rather by Christ's demise. Spared by beauty alone, works will take after, as James instructs. Be that as it may, works are not the premise on which God pardons sin and attributes honesty. This teaching presently can't seem to be genuinely expressed and negated in the Mormon writing.

How at that point do Mormons think that its conceivable to state they have faith in effortlessness alone? Bruce R. McConkie clarifies, "All men are spared by elegance alone with no follow up on their part, implying that they are revived and turned out to be godlike in light of the making amends give up of Christ." Although you might be restored to judgment, your restoration is by effortlessness alone!"

"You might be in torment, however your restoration is by beauty alone! What's more, "all men by the beauty of God have the ability to increase everlasting life. This is called salvation by graces combined with compliance to the laws and mandates of the gospel." Then in the wake of scorning the possibility of Christ's shed blood as the sole ground of absolution, a similar essayist includes, "Salvation in the kingdom of God is accessible as a result of the offering reparations blood of Christ. Be that as it may, it is gotten just on state of confidence, contrition, immersion, and persevering to the end in keeping the precepts of God."

By adding attempts to confidence, Mormons

demolish the very substance of effortlessness. As indicated by Romans 11:6, God's decision of his kin is of beauty," "And if elegance, at that point it is no a greater amount of works: generally effortlessness is no more beauty. Be that as it may, on the off chance that it be of works, at that point it is no more beauty: generally work is no more work." These standards are totally unrelated on the grounds that works get a justified reward yet elegance is spilled out upon the individuals who are undeserving. Effortlessness is outlandish support, the unconditional present of God. The Mormon's endeavored mix of works and confidence uncovers a misconception of both. More than that, it pulverizes the uplifting news. Mormons can not sing, Jesus paid it all, All to Him I owe; Sin had left a dark red stain, He (Jesus) washed it white as snow.

CHAPTER

SIX

Identifying The Cultist:

As Christians, we must understand the gospel of God's grace and to trust in the living Jesus Christ to aid us when in the presence of the "cultist." The essentials of authentic faith reflected in the following seven questions are designed to help the Christian identify a missionary or representative of the cults. Those questions are:

(1) Do you base your teachings on revelations or sacred writings other than the Bible?

(2) Is your primary task preaching the Gospel of Christ? (see I Cor. 15:3-4). The most important business is proclaiming the Gospel – Is it His? There is no other (Gal. 1:8-9)

(3) Do you believe Jesus is the Messiah, the Christ, the anointed one of God who has come in the flesh (I John 4:1-3)? Is Jesus Of Nazareth the Eternal Word of God become flesh? (See John 1:1,14).

Denial of the Lordship of Christ is the spirit of anti-Christ. (see II John 9)

(4) Do you believe Christ's shed blood is the only basis for the forgiveness of sins? (see Romans 3:24-25).

(5) Do you believe that Jesus rose from the dead? (see Romans 10:9-10).

(6) Are you personally trusting Jesus Christ as your Redeemer and Lord? The gospel summons every man to trust his risen Redeemer.

(7) Do you depend upon some achievements of your own for your salvation, or is your trust exclusively in the grace of God? (Not by human achievements or doing good. See Romans and Galatians – that salvation is the gift of God's grace, not by works lest any man should boast. See Ephesians 2:8-9. These questions aid one in not only identifying a "cult" but to guide Christians in evangelizing cultists.

A Sample Questionaire

The following questions alone with prior knowledge of the cultists is very helpful. All cults are to be asked the above questions as well as the questions below. The next chapters render information about other cults, hate groups and counterfeit Christianity. This section of chapter six may be applied to all cultists in the following chapters with adjustments to the knowledge of their group, sect, cult or ism.

1. Gain a knowledge of the teachings of the cultist.
2. What is the cultist teachings on divine authority?
3. Develop your witnessing skills.
4. Does the Cultist accept other beliefs or books outside of the Bible as divine revelation?
5. What can you learn about propagating the faith from the cultist?
6. Does the cultist base their teachings on revelations other than the Bible?
7. List ways in which these revelations fail to fit scriptural facts.

8. List tests of a true prophet and give the cultist a grade of passing or failing.
9. What does the cultist religion teach about the Bible? Or another subject?
10. Set an attitude favorable to helping cultists or hate groups, not embarassisng them.

A. The Gospel:

Question: Is your main business the proclamation of the gospel of Jesus Christ??

B. The Doctrine Of Christ:

Question: Do you believe that Jesus is the Christ, the eternal Word of God who has come in the flesh?

C. Redemption:

Question: Do you believe Jesus Christ died for your sins?

D. The Resurrection Of Jesus Christ:

Question: Do you believe that Jesus Christ rose from the dead bodily?

E. Personal Faith:

Question: Are you personally trusting Jesus Christ as you Redeemer and Lord?

Question: Do you depend upon some achievements of your own to contribute to your justification, or is it only by way of God's grace through faith?

Conclusion

Sum up answers to the cultist's claims of revelation from God in addition to the Bible. Consider ways of presenting the material above to the cultist or hate group.

Note: other questions may arise in witnessing to the cultist. Write them down and explore them.

CHAPTER

SEVEN

Other Counterfeit Christianity and Hate Groups

Christian Science

A faction, the Church of Christ, Scientist, set up in the US by Mary Baker Eddy 1879. Christian Scientist trust that since God is great and is a soul, matter and malevolence are not at last genuine. Thus they all medicinal treatment. It has its own particular every day daily paper, The Christian Science Monitor.

Christian Science is viewed by its followers as the rehashing of primitive Christianity with its full good news of salvation from all abhorrent, including ailment and malady and in addition sin.

As per its disciples, Christian Science recuperating is achieved by the operation of truth in human still, small voice. There is no appointed ministry, however there are open professionals of Christian Science mending who are authoritatively approved.

The Headquarters of the First Church of Christ, Scientist is in Boston, Massachusetts, with branches in many parts of the world. The course book of Christian Science is Eddy's Science and Health with Key to the Scriptures 1875 (Webster's New World Encyclopedia, 1990).

The Church Of God With Signs Following (The Snake Handling Church)

This is additionally referred to by name connected as "Church Of God - With Signs Following" which rehearse wind taking care of and drinking poison amid their love administrations. They attempt to legitimize this practice in light of Mark 16:17-18.

Snake taking care of practice initially showed up in roughly 1910 where it begun in American Christianity under the service of George W. Hensley of Southeastern Tennessee. Hensley was a minister in the Church of God of Richard Spurling - Ambrose J. Tomlinson orgin. Hensley left the congregation with a gathering supporters, shaping a different body known as the snake-taking care of chapel.

This practice started in North Alabama and North Georgia under James Miller. This practice comprises of love benefit comprehensive of supplication, melody, tongues, lecturing and snake - dealing with in the platform or front of the congregation. It is said the snakes spoke to Satan and by permitting snake - taking care of showed one's control over Satan.

The snakes utilized as a part of these love administrations were/and are regularly copperheads, cottonmouths, and poisonous snakes in like manner rehearse; yet at time cobras safe house been utilized. The individuals who feel "Blessed: go to the front of the congregation and handle the snakes; while others may take part in drinking poison (strychnine) as of now. In the event that an individual from a snake - taking care of chapel is nibbled, it is trusted that it is a consequence of absence of confidence or the inability to take after the spirit;s authority. Therapeutic is not looked for after nibbled, but rather individuals accept and seek the Lord for recuperating.

George W. Hensley, a snake dealing with serve kicked the bucket in 1955 in Florida from a harmful snake chomp. Snake dealing with places of worship take after numerous regulations like related Church of God bodies and unmistakable routine with regards to these temples is know differently as "Snake-taking care of, Serpent Handling, and Taking up Serpents.

Islam

Arabic "Submission," that is, to the will of "Allah," religion founded in the Arabian peninsula in the early 7th Century A.D. It emphasizes the oneness of God, his omnipotence, beneficence, and inscrutability. The sacred book is the "Koran" of the prophet Mohammed, the prophet or messenger of Allah. There are two main Muslim sects: The Sunni and The Shiite. Other schools include Sufism, a mystical movement originating in the 8th century.

The belief is that creation, the fall of Adam, Angels and Jinns, heaven and hell, Day of Judgment, God's Predestination of good and evil, and the succession of scriptures revealed to the prophets, including Moses and Jesus, but of which the perfect, final form is the "Koran" or "Quarn," divided into 114 Suras or chapters, said to have been divinely revealed to Mohammed; and the original is said to be presented beside the throne of "Allah." There is no organized church or priesthood, although

Mohamed's descedants (The Hashim Family) and popularly recognized holy men, Mullahs, and Ayatollah are afforded respect.

Islam was seen as an enemy of Christianity by European countries during the crusades, and Christians states united against a Muslim nation as late as battle of Lepanto 1571. Driven from Europe, Islam remained established in North Africa and The Middle East (Webster's New World Encyclopedia, 1988).

Confucianism

This cult, possess a body of beliefs and practices that are based on the Chinese classic and supported by the authority of the philosopher Confucius (Kong Zi).

For about 2,500 years most of the Chinese people have derived from Confucianism their ideas of cosmology, political government, social organization, and individual conduct.

Until 1912, the emperor of China was regarded as father of his people, appointed by heaven to rule. The Superior man was the ideal human and filial piety was the chief virtue. Accompanying a high morality was a kind of ancestor worship (better expressed as reverence/remembrance) remained a regular practice in the home.

The ethical system is based on the teachings of Confucius, emphasizing personal virtue, devotion to family, including the spirits of one's ancestors, and Justice (Webster's New World Encyclopedia, 1990).

Transcendent Meditation (TM)

This is the technique of focusing on the mind, based in part on Hindu Meditation. Meditators are given a Mantra (a special word or phrase) to repeat over and over to themselves; such as meditation is believed to benefit the practitioner by relieving stress and inducing a feeling of well-being and relaxation. It was introduced to the West by Maharishi-Mahesh Yogi; and popularized by the Beatles in the late 1960s (Webster's New World Encyclopedia, 1990).

Buddhism

Originated in India about 500 B. C. It derives from the teachings of Buddha, who is regarded as one of a series of such enlightened beings.

There are no gods. The chief doctrine is that of Karma, good or evil deeds meeting on appropriate reward or punishment either in this life or (through reincarnation) a long succession of lives.

The Buddhist belief is: The self is not regarded as permanent, and the aim of following the Noble Eightfold Path is to break the chain of Karma and achieve dissociation from the body by attaining nirvana ("blowing out") - the eradication of all desires, either in annihilation or by absorption of the self in the infinite.

Supreme reverence is accorded to the historical Buddha, who is seen as one in a long and ongoing line of Buddhas, the next one (Maitreya) due c. AD 3000 (Webster's New World Encyclopedia, 1990).

Jainism

Jainism is a religion founded in the 5th century B. C. by Mahavira (599-527). approximately during the time of Buddhism. Buddhism is the "Middle Way." Jainism is the "most strict religion" with two traditions known as (1) Diganbara (naked) are monks and nuns with a vow of "nudity," usually living in monasteries and (2) "The Suatembara" (white-robed). There are six main rules they follow which include: destroy no life, do not lie, practice charity, practice chastity, possess nothing and want nothing and finally to devote one's whole of life to task (Moshka).

Like Buddhism, it is a rebellion against Hindu life: No gods, no priests, no caste system, but they have the law of Karma or Reincarnation.

They reject thought of any gods of hinduism, but now practically every existing thing is god; the mountains, earth, and stones have a soul; and every plant and animal is a god.

There is no god to help you obtain "Jain," but Mahvira is god, and they have beautiful temples in Calcutta and Mt. Aby in central India is a most holy place.

Jina, the conqueror, the enlightened one, to obtain "Nirvana," Mahavira left his rich home and wandered for 13 years with a Spartan life of denial of all worldly things, even walking nude until enlightened suddenly came to hm after mediatating 2 ½ days under a saia tree on a river bank in Nepal. From Jina comes the name "Jainism" (Webster's New World Encyclopedia, 1990).

CHAPTER

EIGHT

Spiritualism

A faith in survival of the human identity and in the correspondence between the living and the individuals who have "passed on" (perished). The Spiritualist Movement started in the United States in 1848. Followers to this religious section hone "mediumship": which cases to permit "clarivoyant," which claims information of removed occasions and soul mending.

Medium - a person however to have energy to speak with spirits of the dead or specialists of a different universe or measurement.

A person, for example, a medium having the gathered energy of perceptiveness.

Modern Spiritualism

Mysticism communicates tenets of the individuals who trust correspondence between this world and the following is, and dependably has been, a reality. In the seventeenth Century there were many affirmed mystics in France, and a high host of splendid disapproved of people occupied with exploring the different marvels.

The Mesmerist Billot guaranteed that he and his partners had both seen and felt spirits. Delleuze pronounced that the likelihood of speaking with spirits had been demonstrated to him.

Others affirmed that marvels, in all regards indistinguishable with mysticism, showed up in old histories, in the Delphic Oracles, in the occurances of the Wesley Family in 1716, and in Swedenborg asserted full and open correspondence with the soul world and his day by day talk with spirits (Gay Brothers, 1886).

Robert Dale Owen proclaimed that mysticism, as comprehended in the United States, had its introduction to the world around March 31, 1844, when the wonder of soul rapping showed itself to the Fox Family in Hydesville, New York. Different individuals from this family acquired genuine responses to many inquiries by unmistakable raps upon a disengaged table.

Mystics hold that in the event that we concede the likelihood of another existence of which the present is the novitiate, we should likewise concede the probability that implies ought to be offered us to acquire confirmations touching the world for which we need to set ourselves up. They don't have faith in supernatural occurrences, declaring that the common law is all inclusive, constant, relentless, and that all otherworldly epiphanies are normal marvels.

Generally speaking, they don't view Jesus Christ as one of the people in the Godhead. A vast number who might be called "Christian Spiritualists" view Christ with love as the "Incomparable Spiritual and Ethical Teacher of Mankind," while another branch talk about Him as one of the antiquated rationalists, with no claim to qualification past the sages like Confucius, Socrates, or Seneca.

They dismiss the possibility of an individual fallen angel. Some have faith in the intermittent office and impact of malice spirits, producing, from time to time, to what may be called ownership; while others hold that such things may, in all cases, be clarified by human organization. Both, notwithstanding, concur in this: that soul interchanges are in no way, shape or form dependable, and that extraordinary care ought to be taken to acknowledge nothing, come when it might, until it has been submitted to the examination of reason or inner voice (Gay Brothers, 1886).

The Mediums, or people through whom

the interchanges are made, have been isolated as takes after: rapping mediums, mediums for tipping and turning tables by a slight touch of the finger; for the development of awkward bodies without contact; for the generation of bright lights in a dim room; for playing on melodic instruments in a way past their customary capacities, for automatic composition, and for composing autonomous of any guide from human hands, for the diagnosing and mending of sicknesses, for levitation and for the emergence of soul frames indistinguishable in appearance with those of expire people (Gay Brothers, 1886).

Among the main standards on which it might be stated, every canny mystic generously concur are these: This is a world represented by God of affection and benevolence, in which all things cooperate for good of the individuals who respectfully comply with His everlasting laws.

Life proceeds from the life which now is to what is to come. The earth period of life is a basic arrangement for the life which is to come. The period of life which takes after the passing - change is, in the strictest sense, a supplement to what goes before it. Our state here decides our underlying state there.

We don't either by confidence or works win paradise; nor are we sentenced, on any day of anger, to damnation. In the following life we essentially incline toward the position for which, by life on earth, we have fitted ourselves. There is no quick change of character when we go from the present period of life; our resources, interests, ethics, all run over with us.

In the following scene, adore positions higher than what we call insight, acting naturally the most astounding knowledge. These deeds of generosity far exceed callings of confidence (professions of faith) (Gay Brothers, 1886).

As respects the connection of mysticism to the mission of Christ, it might be said that while it votaries more often than not dismiss Trinitarianism and disert from the "Religious philosophy of St. Paul," large portions of the most experienced mystics trust that if otherworldly interchanges be looked for in a sincere, getting to be disposition, the perspectives acquired will, in lion's share of cases, be as per the lessons of Christ. It is stated that Christ Himself guaranteed (John 14:2) that His adherents ought to do works he did, and more prominent works additionally; and further, that there is in purpose of certainty considerable incident between the signs and ponders related in the accounts and the otherworldly epiphanies of the present day.

It is conceded by authentic mystics that a significant number of the correspondences got give off an impression of being an impression of the feelings, proposals, here and there of the medium, in some cases the inquirer; yet it additionally guaranteed that is many cases the answers not just contain data obscure to both, and which is a short time later observed to be valid, yet things and statements absolutely restricted to the feelings of all who hear correspondence (Gay Brothers, 1886).

Mysticism is not viewed as a formal faction; nor do its adherents crave that it ought to end up plainly a different church, with recommended statement of faith, appointed priests, and scholarly teachers.

Its standards are spreading, they accept, as quick as the world can tolerate them understandingly, and in a way the most alluring - to a limited extent through the organization of nearby ministers, yet primarily peacefully through the office of every day intercourse, in the protection of the household circle, attacking the temples officially settled, not as an adversary, but rather as a rear way.

Other than the thousands in each review of society all through the enlightened world, who are pretty much impacted by a faith in heavenly beginning of the indications, numerous people in England, France, Germany, Russia, Switzerland and The United States, recognized in science, writing, reasoning, and statesmanship, have turned out to be declared changes over, or have conceded the

marvels so far as to put stock in another drive not perceived by science, or have seen are not equipped for clarification on the ground of imposture, incident, or

botch, or if nothing else have considered the subject deserving of genuine consideration and watchful investigation(Gay Brothers, 1886).

A Final Word On Spiritualism

Taking everything into account, we should consider the expressions of Dr. Gordon Lewis, from this book, "Going up against the Cults:

"While individuals can not contact spirits of the dead, they can contact underhanded spirits, or evil presences." The devils are not spirits of dead individuals, but rather fallen holy messengers who, in dependability with Satan, war against God (Eph. 6:12).

A young lady who made her lords rich by "divination" at Ancient Philippi was had with an unclean soul (Acts 16:16-18). Their wage was cut off, be that as it may, when in the Name of the Lord Jesus Christ Paul and Silas cast the evil spirit out of her. The pastors of Satan utilize superhuman learning and power for misleading purposes (Rev. 9:20-21; 16:13-14). Nobody focused on Christ and nobility can offer himself to vile reasons for the demon (I Cor. 10:21, Lewis, 1990).

As per Scripture, at that point, the Spiritualist's or (Spiritualism's) principle business is completely mischievous business. Mysticism neglects to announce the "Gospel" to the finishes of the earth. Set up of Our Lord's Great Commission they put counseling spirits. Be that as it may, going up against the transitory outcomes might be, they can not usurp the place of redemptive truth.

Since Satan masks himself as a "holy messenger of light" it is not unusual that his workers likewise camouflage themselves as hirelings of exemplary nature (II Cor. 11:14-15). The Apostle Paul long back "Cautioned" that there is no other gospel, just depravities of Christ's Gospel. Besides, he composed by the Holy Spirit's motivation, "in the event that we, or a holy messenger from paradise," "should lecture you a message in opposition to that gospel, "Let him be damned" (Gal. 1:8-9). One who uproots the gospel with soul messages can not get away from that plain instructing of God's Word. How Urgent, at that point, the Spiritualist's have to turn from the "distorted gospel" to the "One True Gospel" (Lewis, 1990).

CHAPTER

NINE

The Kingdom of Other Cults

Only the Gospel of Jesus Christ has the power and authority over the spirits of deception seen in many counterfeit Christian groups claiming to be churches, lovers of the Gospel, believers of Christ; but only in word (lip service or deceptive ways), but not in thought, heart, nor practice. They oft claim Jesus Christ in belief but deny the power of the gospel thereof. Their doctrines are false and some are simply devilish in nature (come from Satan, of the devil).

Jesus Christ had given us his own blood on Calvary's Cross and the Gospel (His Divine Word) for the believer. He has given the believer the power and authority of the Gospel truly to bind the spirit of deception which misleads, deceives, entraps, leads to hell persons trapped in the kingdom of cults, counterfeit Christianity and hate groups (Matthew 18:18-20).

There exists such an extensive list of cults, sects, isms, hate groups, and other counterfeit groups (far too many to address in this publication) numbering in the thousands across the globe. The devil continues to deploy plots to entrap people throughout the world and in the United States. All Praise be to God The Father through Jesus Christ for the Gospel of Christ in the Holy Bible. Thanks be to God for the Living Word.

Satanism

Accordingly, this term is the "worship of Satan" (Devil Worship), traditionally associated with occultism, witchcraft, and the black mass, black arts. Although some scholars believe that before the 19th century the black mass was largely a literary invention, it has usually been considered the central ritual of "Satanism" (Funk & Wagnalls Encyclopedia, 1983).

The celebrant wears vestments resembling those worn by Christian Priests celebrating mass, except that the chasuble may bear the figure of a goat, an animal often associated with Satan. Other features of the black mass may include the suspension of the cross upside down, parodies and inversions of Christian prayers and creeds, animal sacrifices and ritualistic orgies.

Satanism seems in great part a survival of the worship of demons, for it does not regard worship of Satan as beneficent or ill-treated but as a fiend more powerful than the forces of good, which have been unable to keep the promises they have made to the world.

The history of Satanism is obscure. It is possible that the French Marshal Giles de Rais (1404-1440), who was tried for hersey, satanism, and child murder, was an early adherent. Satanism seems to have been revived during the reign of Louis XIV of France and has maintained itself since that time, usually shrouded in secrecy but occasionally coming to public attention (Funk and Wagnalls Encyclopedia, 1983).

Gnostic Sects

In various Gnostic sects, the serpent was praised as the giver of knowledge, sometimes also Satan with references to his name "Lucifer" or "Light-Bringer."

Some gnostics claimed that being imagined as God by Christians and Jews, by the Gnostics known as the "Demiurge," was in fact "Satan." To some early Gnostics and sects were attributed horrible acts (The Borborites and followers of Carpocrates especially) along with instructions to commit all kinds of evil acts to free themselves from the pains of the world, but such accounts are not generally credible, as they were mostly part of rhetorical attacks against these groups by such heresiological writers as Irenaeus.

Conjurer

A person who claims to be or is believed to possess the ability, power to call up, call on spirits or practices magic.

Necromancy

The art of revealing the future through communicating with the dead (the Black Arts, Maagic, Conjure, Enchantment).

Sorcerer Or Sorceress

A person, male or female witch, wizard, enchanter who uses supernatural power over others through the assistance of evil spirits, witchcraft, black magic.

Warlock

A Male witch, sorcerer, wizard, or demon.

Enchanter

A person belieeved to be a sorcerer, magician. One who practices casting spells or able to cast one under a spell, to charm (a charmer) or one who bewitches.

Obeah

A form of religious belief, probably of African origin, involving witchcraft or sorcery. It is practiced in some parts of the West Indies and nearby Tropical America.

Charmer

One who is put in the same category with idols, those possessing familiar spirits and wizards. They were consulted for advice (scripture speaks against these aforementioned: see Deuteronomy 18:10-12; Isaiah 19:3-4.

Tarot Cards

Fortune-telling aid consisting of 78 cards, the minor Areana in four suits (resembling playing cards) and the major areane, 22 cards with densely symbolic illustrations that have links with Astrology and the Kabbala. It history is unknown (but probably medieval) origin, the earliest known references to tarot cards is from1392. The pack may have been designed in Europe in early 14thy century as repository of Gnostic ideas then being suppressed by the Christian Church. Since the 18th century the tarot has interested occult scholars.

(Webster's New World Encyclopedia, 1990).

Witchcraft
(Inclusive of Black Magic & White Magic)

The alleged possession and exercise magical powers – black magic if used with evil intentions, and white magic if benign. It origins lie in traditional beliefs and religions. Practitioners of witchcraft (Shaman) have often had considerable skill in, for example, herbal medicine and traditional remedies which prompted the World Health Organization in 1976 to recommend the integration of traditional healers into health teams of African States (Webster's New World Encyclopedia, 1990).

The Christian Church persecuted witches in Europe between the 15th and 17th centuries and in North America (Research Salem). The last official execution of a witch in Europe was that of Anna Goddi, hanged in Switzerland in 1782. Obi is the witchcraft of Black Africa imported to the West Indies, and includes Christian elements; Voodoo is a similar cult (Webster's New World Encyclopedia, 1990).

Divination

The art of ascertaining future events or eliciting other hidden knowledge by supernatural or non-rational means. Divination played a large part in the ancient civilization of the Egyptians, Greeks (oracles), Romans and Chinese (I Ching), and is practiced throughout the world.

It generally involves the intuitive interpretation of the mechanical operations of chance or natural law. Forms of divination have omens drawn from the behaviors of birds and animals; examination of the entrails of sacrificed animals; random opening of such books as Bible, fortune-telling by cards (Tarot); and Palmistry, dowsing, oracular trance – speaking; automatic writing; Necromancy, or the supposed raising of the spirits of the dead, and dreams, often specially induced (Webster's New World Encyclopedia, 1990).

Magic

The art of controlling the forces of nature by supernatural means such as charms and rituals. The central idea are that like produces like (sympathetic magic) and that influence carries by contagion or association; for example, by the former principle an enemy could be destroyed through an effigy, by the latter principle through personal items such as hair or nail clippings (witchcraft) (Webster's New World Encyclopedia, 1990).

Occultism

The study of the occult or Hidden Wisdom. Occultism deals with Tailsman, Witchcraft,

Black Arts, Magic, Voodoo, ESP, Lucid Dream and Numerology. Most of what is rejected or unclaimed by any of the major religions is included in the realm of the occult. Some of sorcery, satanism, mysticism, theosophy, anthroposophy and new age (Webster's New World Encyclopedia, 1990).

CHAPTER

TEN

Hate Groups:
The Enemy Threatens

Satan is smart as to impact his malevolent courses upon man not just by means of cliques, fake christian operators, camouflaged as a holy messenger of light, however he additionally betrays through religious false conventions, and detest gatherings. He utilizes these to impact frail casualties with lies or demonaic exercises guaranteeing to be either maintained Christian operators thusly, a positive attitude association, or some other type of religious or social gathering, individual or person. Those endeavors add up to close to malevolent sorted out abhor bunches who have debased either a perspective of Christianity or deny the Bible, have no perspectives or relationship with the Church or Christ by any stretch of the imagination. They frequently despise different races of individuals while turning into a disfavor to their own particular race and society in general; and mistreat people of various foundations, ethnic gatherings, societies, and religion (assuming any) not quite the same as their own convictions; Satan threatens!

Frequently, a large portion of these people confuse the Bible to bolster their mischievous perspectives and use bigotry, racial domination, switched preference, or some other reasoning or conviction remote to Western culture and Christianity. Religious writings, totalitarian belief system, for example, those clung to by Muslim radicals as on account of the Taliban or gatherings, for example, ISIS, or even the Ku Klux Khan are a consistent danger to society and the world in general.

The people who bolster detest gatherings or radicals are no superior to anything the abhor bunches themselves and are at fault similarly so for the impact, financing and different commitments they render to such gatherings in aiding the enemy who threatens (Satan). A portion of the gatherings are The Black Gorilla Family, The Bloods, The Crips, Vice-Lords, Mafia, The Mexican Mafia, Nuestra Family, Neo-Nazis gatherings, Black Gangster Disciples, Neo-Confederates, Christian Identity, Black Separatists, First United Church of Adolf Hitler, Grand Dragon, Racists Action League, The Black Cultists thus a lot of something beyond. In the following chapter we will inform you of the actions of some of the gangs etc which follow.

The Ku Klux Klan

or

The Church Of The American Knights Of The Ku Klux Klan

A US Secret society dedicated to white supremacy, founded 1866 in the Southern US states to oppose Reconstruction after the American Civil War and to deny political rights the black population. Members wore hooded whites robes to hide their identities and burned crosses as a symbol. It was publicized in the 1960s for terrorizing civil-rights activists and organizing racist demonstrations.

It was originally headed by former Confederate general Nathan Bedford Forrest and was disbanded in 1869 under pressure from members who opposed violence. Scattered groups continued a campaign of lynching and flogging, prompting anti-Klan laws in 1871. The group reemerged in 1915 as an anti-Black, anti-Semitic, anti-Catholic, right wing group that portrayed itself as fervently patriotic. Today the Klan has evolved into a paramilitary extremist group that has forged loose ties with other white supremacist groups (Webster's New World Encyclopedia, 1990).

The Church of The American Knights of the Ku Klux Klan, led by Jeff Berry of Butler, Indiana, is the most active Klan organization in America. While other Klan organizations across the country are weakening and becoming less visible, the American Knights are flooding neighborhoods acroos their country with their propaganda and holding rallies in cities from the Midwest to the South (ADL Backgrounder, 2005).

Berry established the American Knights of the KKK in 1995, at a time when other KKK leaders were trying to improve their images by reinventing the Klan as a civic organization for "white people." In contrast, Berry's organization has consistently followed the traditional Klan model, with its cruelty racist literature, it use of vile epithets at public rallies and its combative stance (ADL Backgrounder, 2005).

The organization changed its name to Church

of the American Knights of the Ku Klux Khan (ADL Backgrounder, 2005).

Isalmism

Islamism is a totalitarian ideology adhered to by Muslim Extremist such as ISIS, the Taliban, Hamas and others. It is considered to be a distortion of Islam. Many Islamists engage in terrorism in pursuit of their goals

Islamism is an ideology that demands man's complete adherence to the sacred law of Islam and rejects as much as possible outside influence, with some exceptions such as access to military and medical technology. It is imbused with a deep antagonism towards non-Muslims and has a particular hostility towards the West. It amounts to an effort to turn Islam, a religion and civilization, into an ideology (Pipes, 2015).

The National Alliance

The National Alliance is a Neo-Nazi White Supremacy Organization established by previous American Nazi Party Officer, the Late

Dr. William Pierce (creator of Turner Diaries, kicked the bucket July 23, 2002 - Obituary).

As indicated by the ADL, the National Alliance is the biggest and most dynamic Neo-Nazi association in the United States. Established by the as of late expired - William Pierce and situated in West Virginia, The National's Alliance will likely "form a superior world and a superior race" and to make "another administration"- - responsible to white individuals as it were."

Taking after William Pierce'ws July 23, 202 demise, Erich Gliebe, 39, turned into the National Alliance Chairman. Gliebe considers his war against non-whites "a deep rooted and endless battle," and trusts "it is not vital how" he and his devotees battle the "coming fight," just that they win. He communicated esteem for both remote and household psychological oppressors (apologeticsindex.org, 2005).

Black Separatists

A Black Hate Group consisting of several chapters throughout the United States such as "The Nation of Islam," "The New Black

Panther Party," and "United Nuwabian Nation of Moors." All operate under the umbrella of "Black Separatists."

This racists organization opposes any integration and racial intermarriage. Their ideology is a desire or want for separate nation and institutions for blacks.

They are in most forms strongly anti-white and anti-semetic, and a number religious versions assert that blacks and not Jews are the Biblical "chosen people" of God. Although the Southern Poverty Law Center points out much black racism in America, is at least in part a response to centuries of white racism. Racism must be exposed in all forms, regardless of race, group, religious belief, etc...(US Map of Hate Groups – www.tolerance.org, 2005).

CHAPTER
ELEVEN

A Sample Questionaire

Identifying The Cultist or Hate Group Member:

Note: Apply all questions in chapter 11 to all groups discussed in this book.

As Christians, we must understand the gospel of God's grace and to trust in the living Jesus Christ to aid us when in the presence of the "cultist." The essentials of authentic faith reflected in the following seven questions are designed to help the Christian identify a missionary or representative of the cults and hate groups. Those questions are:

(1) Do you base your teachings on revelations or sacred writings other than the Bible?

(2) Is your primary task preaching the Gospel of Christ? (see I Cor. 15:3-4). The most important business is proclaiming the Gospel – Is it His? There is no other (Gal. 1:8-9)

(3) Do you believe Jesus is the Messiah, the Christ, the anointed one of God who has come in the flesh (I John 4:1-3)? Is Jesus Of Nazareth

the Eternal Word of God become flesh? (See John 1:1,14).

Denial of the Lordship of Christ is the spirit of anti-Christ. (see II John 9)

(4) Do you believe Christ's shed blood is the only basis for the forgiveness of sins?

(see Romans 3:24-25).

(5) Do you believe that Jesus rose from the dead? (see Romans 10:9-10).

(6) Are you personally trusting Jesus Christ as your Redeemer and Lord? The gospel summons every man to trust his risen Redeemer.

(7) Do you depend upon some achievements of your own for your salvation, or is your trust exclusively in the grace of God? (Not by human achievements or doing good. See Romans and Galatians – that salvation is the gift of God's grace, not by works lest any man should boast. See Ephesians 2:8-9. These questions aid one in not only identifying a "cult" but to guide Christians in evangelizing cultists.

A Sample Questionaire

The following questions alone with prior knowledge of the cultists (Or Hate Group Member) is very helpful. All cults/Hate Group Members are to be asked the above questions as well as the questions below.

1. Gain a knowledge of the teachings of the cultist.
2. What is the cultist teachings on divine authority?
3. Develop your witnessing skills.
4. Does the Cultist accept other beliefs or books outside of the Bible as divine revelation?
5. What can you learn about propagating the faith from the cultist?
6. Does the cultist base their teachings on revelations other than the Bible?
7. List ways in which these revelations fail to fit scriptural facts.
8. List tests of a true prophet and give the cultist a grade of passing or failing.
9. What does the cultist religion teach about the Bible? Or another subject?

10. Set an attitude favorable to helping cultists or hate groups, not embarassisng them.

A. The Gospel:
Question: Is your main business the proclamation of the gospel of Jesus Christ??

B. The Doctrine Of Christ:
Question: Do you believe that Jesus is the Christ, the eternal Word of God who has come in the flesh?

C. Redemption:
Question: Do you believe Jesus Christ died for your sins?

D. The Resurrection Of Jesus Christ:
Question: Do you believe that Jesus Christ rose from the dead bodily?

E. Personal Faith:
Question: Are you personally trusting Jesus Christ as you Redeemer and Lord?

Question: Do you depend upon some achievements of your own to contribute to your justification, or is it only by way of God's grace through faith?

Conclusion

Sum up answers to the cultist's/Hate Group Member claims of revelation from God in addition to the Bible (if any). Consider ways of presenting the material above to the cultist or hate group.

Note: other questions may arise in witnessing to the cultist. Write them down and explore them.

For Further Study

Below are a few publications which will aid in your understanding cults and your study of them:

Anthony A. Hoekema. The Four Major Cults. Grand Rapids, MI: Eerdmans Publishing Company, 1963

Marcus Bach. The Unity Way Of Life. Englewood Cliffs, New Jersey" Prentice- Hall, 1962

Larry W. Jonas. Mormon Claims Examined. Grand Rapids, MI: Baker Book House, 1961

Walter R. Martin & Norman H. Klann. Jehovah of the Watchtower. Grand Rapids, MI: Zondervan Publishing House

BIBLIOGRAPHY

American Heritage Dictionary Of English Languaage (1982). William Morris Editor. Boston, Mass.: Houghton Miffin Company

Baalen, J. K. Van (1962) The Chaos Of The Cults -4th Edition. Grand Rapids, MI.: William B. Eerdmans Publishing Company

Church Of The American Knights Of The Ku Klux Klan (2005) Retrieved March 3, 2005 from www.adl.org

Funk & Wagnalls New Encyclopedia (1983) New York, NY.: Funk & Wagnalls

Haagar, G. J. (1886) What The World Believes -The False And The True. New York, NY.: Gay Brothers & Company

Hoekema, A. A. (1963) The Four Major Cults. Grand Rapids, MI.: William B. Eerdmans Publishing Company

Hyatt, J. P. (1977) The Heritage Of Biblical Faith. Saint Louis, MO.: The Bethany Press

Lewis, G. R. (1990) Confronting The Cults. Grand Rapids, MI.: Baker Book House

Lindsa y, G. (1972) Satan's Rebellion And Fall. Dallas, TX.: Christ For The Nations

Lexicon Universal Encyclopedia (1988) "Mormons" USA: Lexicon Publications, Inc

Martin, W. R. (1965) The Kingdom Of The Cults. Grand Rapids, MI,: Zondervan Publishing Company

Neve, J. L. (1944) Churches And Sects Of Christendom. Blair, NEB.: Lutheran Publishing House

New World Translation Of The Holy Scripture (1961) Brooklyn, NY.: Watchtower Bible & Tract Society

Pipes, D. (2015) Nothing Abides: Perspective Of The Middle East & Islam. New Brunswick, USA.: London, UK.: Transaction Publishers

The Theory Of Evolution (2004) Retrieved October 21, 2009 from www.was.darwin,com

The Holy Bible (1964) Authorized King James Version. Chicago, Ill.: J. G. Ferguson

The Holy Bible (2000) The Adventure Bible-The New International Version. Grand Rapids, MI.: Zondervan (used by permission)

The National Alliance (2005) Retrieved February 10, 2005 from www.apologeticsindex.org

Thompson, C. J. (1978) The Miracle Of Salvation. Philadelphia, PA.: Dorrance

US Map of Hate Groups (2005) Black Separatists. Retrieved March 15, 2005 from www. tolerance.org

Webster's New World Encyclopedia (1990) 1st Prentice Edition. New York, NY.: Random Century Group

White, E. G. (1988) The Great Controversy. 2nd Edition Beersheba, TN,: Harvestime Books

ABOUT THE AUTHOR

The Reverend Dr. John Thomas Wylie is one who has dedicated his life to the work of God's Service, the service of others; and being a powerful witness for the Gospel of Our Lord and Savior Jesus Christ. Dr. Wylie was called into the Gospel Ministry June 1979, whereby in that same year he entered The American Baptist College of the American Baptist Theological Seminary, Nashville, Tennessee.

As a young Seminarian, he read every book available to him that would help him better his understanding of God as well as God's plan of Salvation and the Christian Faith. He made a commitment as a promising student that he would inspire others as God inspires him. He understood early in his ministry that we live in times where people question not only who God is; but whether miracles are real, whether or not man can make a change, and who the enemy is or if the enemy truly exists.

Dr. Wylie carried out his commitment to God, which has been one of excellence which led to his earning his Bachelors of Arts in

Bible/Theology/Pastoral Studies. Faithful and obedient to the call of God, he continued to matriculate in his studies earning his Masters of Ministry from Emmanuel Bible College, Nashville, Tennessee & Emmanuel Bible College, Rossville, Georgia. Still, inspired to please the Lord and do that which is well – pleasing in the Lord's sight, Dr. Wylie recently on March 2006, completed his Masters of Education degree with a concentration in Instructional Technology earned at The American Intercontinental University, Holloman Estates, Illinois. Dr. Wylie also previous to this, earned his Education Specialist Degree from Jones International University, Centennial, Colorado and his Doctorate of Theology from The Holy Trinity College and Seminary, St. Petersburg, Florida.

Dr. Wylie has served in the capacity of pastor at two congregations in Middle Tennessee and Southern Tennessee, as well as served as an

Evangelistic Preacher, Teacher, Chaplain, Christian Educator, and finally a published author, writer of many great inspirational Christian Publications such as his first publication: ***"Only One God: Who Is He?" – published August***

2002 via formally 1ˢᵗ books library (which is now AuthorHouse Book Publishers located in Bloomington, Indiana & Milton Keynes, United Kingdom) which caught the attention of **The Atlanta Journal Constitution Newspaper.**

Printed in the United States
By Bookmasters